℞ipley

PUBLISHING

Publishing Director Anne Marshall
Editorial Director Becky Miles
Art Director Sam South
Senior Designer Michelle Foster
Assistant Editor Charlotte Howell
Designer Ark Creative
Reprographics Juice Creative

Published by Scholastic Inc. SCHOLASTIC and associated logos are trademarks and/or
registered trademarks of Scholastic Inc., 557 Broadway, New York , NY 10012

For information regarding permission, write to VP Intellectual Property,
Ripley Entertainment Inc.,
Suite 188, 7576 Kingspointe Parkway, Orlando, Florida 32819
email: publishing@ripleys.com

ISBN 978-0-545-38075-1

12 11 10 9 8 7 6 5 4 3 2 1   11 12 13 14 15/0

Printed in the U.S.A.
First printing, September 2011

PUBLISHER'S NOTE

While every effort has been made to verify the accuracy of the entries in this book,
the Publisher cannot be held responsible for any errors contained in the work.
They would be glad to receive any information from readers.

WARNING

Some of the stunts and activities in this book are undertaken by experts and should
not be attempted by anyone without adequate training and supervision.

shout outs

Ripley's——
Believe It or Not!

ROAR!

CRAZY ANIMAL STORIES

LICK
LICK LICK

?

Illustrated by
John Graziano

INTRODUCING...
JOHN GRAZIANO

John, Ripley's very own cartoonist, has drawn every cartoon in this wacky book of animal stories and facts.

A new Ripley's cartoon has been produced every day for the past 90 years by a dedicated Ripley's cartoonist. John is only the eighth person to take on this role. Amazingly, he got himself the job 25 years after sending his drawings to Ripley's as a teenager!

SPEEDY QUESTIONS!

1. Q: What tools do you use for your drawings?
A: My actual drawings are done the old-fashioned way: with pencil, pen and ink, brush and ink to paper. For airbrushing and coloring, I use a Wacom digital tablet.

2. Q: If you hadn't become an artist, what would you be?
A: I actually wanted to be a paleontologist and dig up fossils! I do that as a hobby though.

3. Q: Which of the animal stories made you laugh out loud?
A: Probably the one about the "Doggie Day Camp!"

4. Q: What is your favorite animal?
A: Doggies!

HOW TO DRAW A...
FISH BOWL

1. Let's start with a circle. Use a pencil so you can erase the lines that you don't want later on. Don't worry if it's not perfect. Make it as round as you can. This will be the goldfish bowl.

2. "Stack" two flat oval shapes on top of the circle. Draw a squiggly line at the bottom of the bowl like this. Add a few "dots" as well to show the sandy bottom.

3. Everything around us is built from shapes. Here you can see circles, triangles, and rectangles. These shapes make up the form of our funny little goldfish.

4. Draw around the shapes and you will see a form of the fish start to appear. Then erase all the lines you now don't need.

5. Add a circle with two little triangles in the sandy bottom like this. This will be a seashell. Add some scales to your fish and a half-circle for his gill.

6. Draw some lines on the seashell and on the fins of the goldfish. Add another gill if you like. How about some personality? Draw an eyebrow above the eye. He sure looks happy in his little bowl! Practice until you are happy with your drawing. Try some different shapes and see what kind of fish you can make!

ROAR!

animals

I'M SO HUNGRY!

You won't believe the wacky things animals do when you dip inside this fun-packed book! Meet Brutus the skydiving dog, Sidney the not-so-speedy snail, and Houdini the greedy snake who bit off more than he could chew, plus many more!

It's Ripley's Shout Outs!

TRUMPETY TRUMP

Now you can download a Jumbo: The Thai Elephant Orchestra is made up of a group of Indian elephants, all playing instruments, and they have even released their own CDs! The elephants have their own giant drums, cymbals, xylophones, and other percussion instruments. One CD has sold over 7,000 copies in the U.S.A. alone!

Tarantulas hunt at night, feasting on animals such as frogs, birds, and lizards. They crush prey with their large fangs.

A snake can sleep with both eyes open.

Love bird

A poor swan in Hamburg, Germany, fell head-over-wings in love with a swan-shaped pedal boat and followed it around. He was so in love that he used to get jealous of anyone who went near the boat.

Deputy camel

Believe it or not, Bert the Camel was successfully sworn in as a Sheriff's Deputy! The six-year-old camel was appointed to serve his Sheriff at a local festival in San Dimas, California.

Reggie was a baby baboon born in a zoo in Devon, England. He was fine until...

LICK LICK LICK

...his mom licked all the hair from the top of his head!

She just wanted to keep him well-groomed...

SNIFF!

...but Reggie ended up with no hair at all!

Luckily, his mom and the other baboons still totally accepted him in their group.

Rat racers

Boomer Hodel, a teenage surfer and rat-owner from Hawaii, combined his hobbies and taught his pets to ride the waves! His two rats named Fin and Tofu took to the water instantly when he took them to the beach. Now they have their own mini surfboards, and can cope with waves 4 feet high!

TOTALLY FAR OUT DUDE!

Ripley's MIGHTY MOUSE

This venomous viper met its match when a lure mouse was put in its cage as a snack but instead attacked the 14-inch-long snake and killed it after a half-hour battle to the death!

GRUMBLE

I'M SO HUNGRY!

Pythons wrap their scaly bodies around their prey until they suffocate—gross!

Road chill

Imagine the shock you would have if you saw a frozen cat at the side of the road! That's just what happened to Roberta Johnson in Minnesota, who spotted a cat's face peeping out of an ice block. She took it to the veterinarian, who gently defrosted the animal and confirmed it was fine apart from having frostbitten ears.

MEOWCH!

It's thought the cat had fallen asleep on the tire of a car, become frozen, and fallen out of the wheel well as the car drove off!

CRAZY CREATURES...

Giant gulp

The sperm whale can hold its breath for up to an hour and a half to dive deep in search of food.

Stomach stamina

Siberian tigers have a massive appetite. They can eat 100 pounds of meat in one meal—that's the same as eating 400 burgers!

Heads up

Even though a giraffe's neck is really long, it still has only seven bones—the same number as in a human's neck.

Lucky chickies

Ever heard of rose-colored glasses? You're said to be wearing them if you have a happy outlook on life. But cheery chickens on a farm in Canada are actually wearing them! Specially designed pink glasses have been found to make the birds calmer and less likely to peck at one another. That's truly living in a rose-tinted world!

Half-awake

A dolphin sleeps with one eye open and one eye closed.

All mixed up! The crayfish has teeth in its stomach and its liver in its head.

King penguins are super-social—as many as 600,000 live together.

One hump or two?

Camels can have one or two humps on their back. Dromedaries have one (like a D) and Bactrian camels have two (like a B).

Not so dull diet

Koalas eat only the leaves and bark of eucalyptus trees, but the different species of eucalyptus taste very different to them, like the different flavors in an ice-cream parlor.

Fast-food

What's the fastest fish in the ocean? The sailfish, which reaches top speeds of 70 mph.

Stoat, look, listen

Clever baby animals in Britain have found a safe way to cross a busy road. Instead of making a run for it across the lanes of traffic, they get where they're going through an underground network of drainage tunnels. A baby stoat and rabbit are regular users, and a pair of baby owls were seen hiding at the drain's entrance while they waited for food.

HUNGRY HOUDINI

What would you do if you were cold and hungry? A snake called Houdini had one solution—eat an electric blanket! The

12-FOOT-LONG

pet python didn't actually plan to picnic on the blanket, but was trying to get to his actual food—a rabbit—that was wrapped up inside. Houdini had to be taken to the pet clinic in Idaho, where X-rays revealed that he had swallowed electric wires AND the heating unit of the blanket, and the wires went right through

8 FEET

of the snake's insides!

It can take a snake days to digest a large animal. That's a long meal!

ZAP

ZAP!

Veterinarians managed to remove the electric blanket, and Houdini made a complete recovery.

Happy snappy

Look after your teeth: Once your first set have fallen out, you're stuck with the next set for the rest of your life. That's not the case with alligators, which have between

2,000 AND 3,000 TEETH

in their lifetime. A full set is made up of around 80 teeth, which are replaced when they break or become worn down.

Fishy tale

Where's the goldfish gone? When a fish disappeared from the pond of Craig and Julie Struthers in New Zealand, they feared the worst, until it was found five days later swimming in a roadside ditch. It had been washed away in a flash flood, and dumped in a ditch over a mile down the road!

RIPLEY's
BEAR-BACK RIDING

It seems that Juan, an Andean spectacled bear, was so desperate to escape from the Berlin Zoo, Germany, that he hatched a complicated plan.

First, he paddled across the moat using a log as a raft.

Then, after climbing the wall of his enclosure...

...he found a bicycle leaning against the railings and may well have ridden off...

if he hadn't been tranquilized by zoo keepers and taken back to safety.

WANTED!
HENRY THE CAT

CRIME: THEFT

LOCATION: LOUGHBOROUGH, ENGLAND

Henry is not your ordinary cat burglar. He steals... socks! So far he has purr-loined 85 socks (plus a pair of underpants and several gloves). His owner, Louise Brandon, thinks he steals the socks from their neighbors' clotheslines, and has a sackful to return if anyone can provide a matching half to a pair.

Animals that live in caves adapt to their underground life. Cave fish never come out, so they are pale and usually blind.

Dung roamin'

The frogs of Sri Lanka's Bundala National Park like to live in elephant poop! They usually live in leaf litter, but when that is hard to find in the dry season, they move home into the plentiful elephant droppings that lie on the ground.

Jellyfish have no brain, heart, bones or eyes, and are around 95 percent water—yet they can still sting with their tentacles!

Massive mount

A pony measuring over 58 inches is classed as a horse. A horse measuring 79½ inches tall is classified as a giant! That's the size of a Belgian draft horse owned by Bill Priefert of Texas. Goliath is 79½ inches from floor to shoulder and weighs

2,400 POUNDS!

He drinks 20 gallons of water and eats 40 pounds of hay and 18 pounds of grain every day.

Fast flyer

How fast can a duck fly? Fast enough to set off a traffic radar camera! Road officials checking the photographs of speeding motorists were amazed to see a picture of a duck. No speed was recorded, but it had flown past fast enough to trigger the radar.

Some domestic cats weigh as much as a five-year-old child.

SHEEP DOG

When is a sheep dog not a sheep dog? When it's just a sheep! Emlyn Roberts has noticed that one of his sheep likes to herd ducks, watch TV with its owner, and loves being taken for a walk on a leash. The sheep also enjoys sliding down a ramp, just like the sheepdogs it was raised with.

Milking machine

In the town of Carnation, Washington, there once lived a cow that produced 3,739 gallons of milk in just one year! The cow—who is commemorated with her own life-size statue—also churned out a whopping 2,865 pounds of butter. That's ten times the yearly amount produced by the average cow, and a lot of milk bottles!

UDDERLY EXHAUSTED!

Walking on water

No, it's not a miracle—but it is pretty amazing. A reservoir in Pennsylvania has such a large number of carp in its waters that the local ducks can walk right across them without getting their webbed feet wet!

GRAZIANO

A queen termite (white ant) can lay 80,000 eggs in a day.

BEYOND BELIEF

Fangs for that

The viperfish is a ferocious predator that lives deep in the world's oceans. It has enormous fang-like teeth that stick out way beyond its mouth and even past its eyes. Yikes! If human teeth were as large in comparison, your bottom teeth would grow to 12 inches past your nose!

Spider supper

The Goliath bird-eating tarantula is so big that if it were served up for your supper its legs would hang over the edge of your plate!

Sweaty feet

An elephant has no pores in its skin, so it cannot sweat in the same way as a human. Instead, it sweats between its giant toenails. Most elephants have 18 toenails, and those few that have 20 toenails are said to be a sign of good luck.

Refrigerator gators

Certain types of alligator spend the winter frozen in the ice, with only their nose sticking out so they can breathe.

If you gathered all the ants in the world together, they would weigh more than all the people on Earth!

Golf tea

Bertie the dog was walking in a most peculiar way, so his owners took him to be examined by a veterinarian. The animal doctor found out what was wrong: Bertie had eaten nine golf balls and they were still in his stomach!

Mighty mites

Dust is made up of dead skin and hair. If that's not gross enough, it's full of dust mites—millions in every ounce of the stuff. Ugh!

Chicken penguin

Kentucky, a Humboldt penguin at a zoo in England, is afraid of water! The rest of his penguin pals regularly take the plunge and go for a swim, but Kentucky stands on the edge to watch. His keepers think his small size and lack of feathers mean he feels the cold too much to dive in.

Orangutans get the most from their forest homes, using leaves as toilet paper, bedding, napkins, and umbrellas.

BAD HAIR-LIFE

Poor old Whipper is a birdie with a difference. His extremely rare "feather duster" syndrome makes his feathers grow so long and curly that he looks like a cuddly toy. The bundle of fluff cannot see or fly, and his parents were so shocked by the way he looks, they tried to get rid of him twice! Luckily, he was rescued, and now gets plenty of visitors who can't believe their eyes when they see him.

Stick insects are so eager to stay camouflaged that they will even shed their legs to look more stick-like. Young stick insects grow new legs soon after.

Greedy guts

An 18-foot python was causing a road block in Malaysia and had to be moved by firefighters to free up the traffic. The snake had eaten a pregnant sheep, and became too full to move by itself. A python can dislocate its jaws to

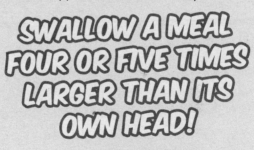

SWALLOW A MEAL FOUR OR FIVE TIMES LARGER THAN ITS OWN HEAD!

An octopus is so squishy it can squeeze through a hole the size of its eyeball.

DO THE CATERPILLAR

You might think that the caterpillar is a dance move done by humans, but the larvae of the birch sawfly think differently. These caterpillars rock a group dance routine that helps keep them safe from predators. Half a dozen of them together rear up on their back legs and dance in the air to make them look too scary to eat. That leaves the others safe to keep on munching.

freaky beak

The kiwi is instantly recognizable as the national bird of New Zealand. It is squat, round, has feathers like whiskers, and

NOSTRILS ON THE END OF ITS BEAK!

These give it a great sense of smell to sniff out the hundreds of worms it eats every night.

The giant anteater eats around 3,000 ants and termites every day.

Flap, flap, woof

The state insect of California is the dogface butterfly, with distinctive yellow-and-black wing markings. Look closely and you'll see the outline of a yellow "poodle's head" on each forewing, with a black dot forming the "eye" of the dog. California was the first state to select a state insect, in 1929, and currently 42 states have a chosen insect.

Some bats fly as high as 10,000 feet chasing moths—that's the height of a parachute jump.

Speedycat

A poor tabby named Hutchinson got the ride of its life when its owner set off with the cat on the roof of her car. Torri Hutchinson, of Idaho, didn't know the cat was there until another motorist signaled to her that something was wrong and she should pull over. She had driven 10 miles along the highway, and not even noticed Hutchinson when she stopped for gas!

Mail attachment

A carrier pigeon with a memory card strapped to its leg delivered its message faster than an Internet download!

THE BIRD FLEW 50 MILES

across South Africa in 1 hour 8 minutes. The same data was downloaded and took just over two hours to transfer from computer to computer.

RIPLEY's
ANT AMBUSH

Amazonian tree ants are not to be messed with. These clever critters make a trap from fungus and tiny plant hairs, then lie in wait in small holes inside. They can capture prey that is MASSIVE compared to their own size: When it crawls onto the trap they pin it down by its legs, wings, and antennae, and then set their worker ants on it to sting it to death.

The prey walks across the tree unaware of what lurks below...

Desert locusts are only the size of a paper clip, but billions of them can swarm together and munch thousands of tons of food every day.

...until the Amazonian tree ants strike, taking their prey by surprise!

There is no escape now! The ants sting their prey to death. Ouch!

Ssss-bend

Yikes! Here's one to watch out for: A snake was found living in the sewer system of a British apartment block! The

10-FOOT BOA CONSTRICTOR

was first seen in a toilet bowl, but when firefighters were called in, it had disappeared back down the bowl. The snake eventually showed up on the floor of another bathroom in the same block.

CRITTER KINGDOM...

Feathered heads

Bald eagles aren't bald...they have feathers on their head like other eagles, and their name comes from an Old English word meaning "white."

AMAZING!

In a flap

Is it a bird? Is it a plane? No, it's a cat with wings! The unusual kitty was born in China and looked normal to begin with, but began to sprout wing-like growths on its back when it was a year old. Scientists aren't sure why this happened.

Scared of spiders? Get over it! Scientists think there is always one within 3 feet, wherever you are.

Rodents' revenge

Dogs love to chase rabbits and squirrels, but should learn a lesson from "Piper." The stray dog from Texas got its nickname after it chased one rabbit too many, and got its head stuck in a 4-foot-long pipe. Fort Worth Animal Control came to the rescue, and managed to get Piper's head unstuck using mineral oil.

INCREDIBLE!

Whale bait

Tiny shrimp-like krill, the fave food of giant whales, live in groups of up to 60,000 called swarms. Around 7,500 krill could live in just one bathtub of water.

Cu l8ter

Elephants can send text messages! Not by typing with their huge toes— obviously—but with a special SIM card fixed onto a collar. It's part of a project in Kenya to stop the elephants from walking too near to private farmland. Park rangers receive a text message when the elephant strays too close to the fence so they can bring it back to safety.

A blue whale has such a big tongue that 50 people could stand on it at the same time!

Bionic bugs

A single leaf cutter ant, measuring only half an inch long, can carry a piece of leaf 20 times heavier than itself. That's the same as your dad carrying a small car!

Sea wings

A manta ray's pectoral (side) fins are up to 23 feet wide and look like wings.

JUMBO PAINTING

Not only a huge picture, but one painted by elephants! The animals at Maesa Elephant Camp in Thailand are talented trunk artists, and have even sold their work at the famous Christie's auction house raising $50,000. The biggest picture was created by eight artistic elephants, each of them holding a brush with the end of their trunk.

The crazy balloon frog of Mexico floats across the water by ballooning to three times its size.

Down in the mouth

A broken beak could have meant the end for a hornbill nicknamed Metal Mickey at Birdland in England as he could easily have

STARVED TO DEATH.

His clever keepers, however, managed to make him a new beak from stainless steel!

Doggy 'do

Nope—nothing to do with poop, but hairdos for dogs. Owners who want to 'do up their dogs can now buy wigs for their pampered pooches. Some of the best-selling styles include the "Yappy Hour," which is a fluffy, curly wig, and the "Peek a Bow Wow," which drapes over the dog's face in a glamorous movie-star style.

Who's been sitting in my chair?

Imagine the surprise of a woman in West Vancouver, Canada, when she walked into her kitchen and found a bear eating porridge! Her name wasn't Goldilocks, but the bear was munching on a container of oatmeal it had found. The lady called the police and it took three officers to remove the bear to safety.

A hungry polar bear can sniff out a seal that is 20 miles away.

Brazil's barking toad really does make a barking noise. It has horns on its eyes, and its bite will kill a large mammal.

Do you take this chimp?

A wedding with a difference has taken place at Rio de Janeiro zoo in Brazil.

TWO CHIMPANZEES

who were brought together to breed

GOT MARRIED!

The couple spent four months in separate cages, flirting and getting to know each other. On their big day, they wore wedding clothes and had a large wedding cake.

The biggest African elephants can eat a whopping 350 pounds of food each day. That's the weight of two large men.

IT'S A DOG'S LIFE

It isn't easy taking care of a pet 24-7, but some dog owners can take a break by sending their dogs to a kind of boot camp. The Doggie Day Camp takes place near Bogotá, the capital of Colombia.

DOGGIE CAMP

PADDLE POOL

Excited mutts board the colorful bus to a nearby village, where their whole day is spent playing sports. They play tennis and soccer, swim doggy paddle in the pool, and lose a few pounds on the treadmill, before they head home. Most of them are exhausted and have a dognap on the way back!

HORN OF PLENTY

The Watusi steer, a type of cattle from Africa, is a medium-sized cow with XXXL horns. Generally, Watusi horns reach 6 feet long, and are filled with blood vessels that help to keep the cows cool. One famous Watusi was Lurch, whose horns exceeded expectations at an amazing 7½ feet long and 38 inches around!

School trip

A school of catfish once went for a walk along a Florida street. The catfish, which can live out of water for a short time in moist conditions, crawled out of a flooded sewer and used their pectoral (side) fins to pull themselves along through the rain.

The bootlace worm is one of the world's longest creatures, growing up to 180 feet in length.

The three-toed sloth hangs upside down in a tree, and only leaves to use the toilet. It's so slow it would take an hour to finish a 100-meter race.

HOT DIGGETY DOG!

Yes, you can believe your eyes: It's a dog riding a motorbike! The Dalmatian lives in the Chinese city of Nanjing, and can be seen on its motorcycle and sidecar, wearing shades, coolly riding around town. Its owner says it can travel around 650 feet at 5 mph. It can even steer in the right direction.

BEEP BEEP!

Donkey dollars

A donkey who was short of money walked into a bank in France with his owner and was able to cash a check by "signing" it with an inked hoof-mark.

EUCH!

Tongue muncher

Gross, gross, and
more gross: There's
a type of parasite that
destroys a fish's tongue and
lives in the fish's mouth in its
place! The parasite is a crustacean
(like a shrimp) called *Cymothidae exigua*. It grows to be
about 1½ inches long, and gains entry through the fish's
gills. Then it cuts off the blood supply so the tongue dies,
and lurks in the fish's mouth, feeding on the fish's blood
and mouth juices.

SPECIAL DELIVERY

Traveling the world is great—but doing it by mail isn't the best way to see the sights. Janosch the cat, belonging to Gitti Rauch in Germany, crawled into a box for a nap and was boxed up and mailed out by mistake. Two days and 450 miles later, mail workers noticed the package move. It was opened and the cat crawled out unharmed.

Ouch!

More people are killed by honeybees every year than are killed by all the poisonous snakes in the world put together. In Australia alone, around ten deaths each year result from honeybee stings. Snakes bite only in self-defense, and most bites can now be treated with anti-venom.

RIPLEY's ROCKET POWERED

Super snails take part in the only official World Snail Racing Championship in Norfolk, England. The snails slime their way from the start line at the center of a circle, and the first past the outer circle is the winner. Although the world record time is 2 minutes, the 2010 winner, Sidney, crept across in a very respectable 3 minutes and 41 seconds. He was fed rocket lettuce beforehand, which might be the key to his speed! If only he'd eaten more of it!

1st

Limp-along

Elephants can live to be over 70 years of age, but they show signs of growing older, just like people.

A 98-YEAR-OLD ELEPHANT

named Malai broke her leg in 2005, and had to be put in a bamboo leg splint to help the injury heal.

POP

Every zebra has its own unique pattern of stripes.

POP GOES THE... HEDGEHOG

Okay, so in the nursery rhyme it's a weasel that goes pop, but in real life, Michelin the hedgehog became so swelled up, a veterinary nurse had to bring him back down to size with a needle. A rare condition caused the prickly patient to swell up like a balloon, but three hours after treatment he was back to his usual self.

WHOOOSH

Scientists have discovered a species of octopus that can walk on two legs! The tiny tropical species curls into a ball, and then pokes out two of its eight tentacles to "walk" along the ocean floor. Oddly enough, the walking style makes the octopus move backward instead of forward.

An ant has five noses for different sorts of smells.

Cubic poo

The Australian marsupial, the wombat, has droppings in the shape of dice! It poops up to 100 of these cubes a day, and the unusual shape stops the pellets from rolling away and making more of a mess. So watch where you're walking and you'll keep clean feet AND know if there's been a wombat around!

ANIMAL ANTICS...

Shark tale

The enormous whale shark is the world's biggest species of fish. In 1912, one was caught that measured 45 feet long, 23 feet 9 inches around, and weighed 30,000 pounds. It took 39 hours to catch and land the beast.

HUGE!

Mini mammal

The smallest bat in the world is the Kitti's hog-nosed bat, which weighs only as much as a dime.

Lifting a leg

A Russian terrier named Ringo has been trained to kickbox. His owner is a former world champion kickboxer, and has taught Ringo to jump up and kick with his two front legs. Apparently, he can deliver a knockout paw-punch on command!

INCREDIBLE!

Speed drinker

A dromedary camel can walk for 100 miles across a desert without drinking. When it does find water, it can gulp down 30 gallons in 13 minutes.

AMAZING!

> Cute little geckos are stronger than they look—they can support their entire body weight using just one toe!

Great grazers

Forget about lawn mowers—buy a wallaby! Around 3 feet tall and as cute as you like, they love to munch on grass and will happily graze all night long, keeping the lawn neat and tidy for their owners. However, be warned—they eat anything green and tasty, so your flowerbeds may be as well trimmed as your grass...

In the bug corner

Male stag beetles use their antlers to fight each other. The winner is the one who flips the other onto its back.

Day trippers

Some apes, such as orangutans and bonobos (a kind of chimpanzee) prepare the things they need if they are going on a trip. They pack up the tools they use to get their food, such as special sticks and stones. So if you see an orangutan carrying a backpack, you know what's inside!

> Snails can sleep for surprisingly long periods—up to three years at a time!

SCORING A CAT-TRICK

Step right up! Come and watch fantastic felines perform amazing tricks at Yuri Kuklachev's Moscow Cats Theater. See around 30 trained housecats in a "pawfect pawformance."

BALANCING ACTS

TIGHTROPE WALKING

UPSIDE DOWN!

FRONT PAW STANDS

Believe it or not, two Austrian designers have come up with clothes for chickens. The suits are available in different colors and patterns, from hairy and knitted to camouflage and the Austrian flag. A special Japanese flag design was shown on a Japanese catwalk at the 2005 World Expo where, unfortunately, one of the models made a chicken poop on the runway.

MONKEY BUSINESS

Whiplash is a capuchin cowboy! The tiny monkey has been riding since he was two, and has learned to herd sheep while sitting astride his sheepdog steed. He performs at over 100 rodeo shows a year, and can outmaneuver many human riders with his skills in the saddle.

YEE-HA!

Clever twist

Octi the octopus, living in the National Aquarium of New Zealand, has a handy trick for

WHEN IT'S HUNGRY.

It can hold a bottle or jar in its tentacles, and use one of the remaining tentacles to twist off the lid and reach the food inside.

ROAD RATS

Calling all four-legged speed demons!
Bored hamsters and gerbils can now own
their own four wheels, in the shape of
the "Critter Cruiser." The tiny car is
paw-powered and lets pets zoom
around on the floor, or on a specially
designed racetrack. It can be set to rotate
on the spot too, if you're getting fed up
with being run over by your rodent.

Worldwide web

A parked car in Rotterdam, Netherlands, was

MYSTERIOUSLY COVERED

from hood to trunk in strange, sticky white stuff.
Its driver discovered that the covering was the
silken web of the

ERMINE MOTH CATERPILLAR.

These larvae often work together to spin
a communal web, in preparation for turning
into fully formed moths. The gangs of hundreds
of caterpillars can spin enough silk to cover cars
and even whole trees!

The Australian glass eel is virtually see-through. You could still read this page if a glass eel were lying on it.

Jumping jack

A little terrier from Wales has been banned from his local darts tournaments because he won't leave the darts in the board. He can easily reach the bull's-eye in a single leap, and sometimes leaps over 6 feet to steal darts from the top of the board.

MAN'S BEST FRIEND

Brutus the dachshund loves his owner so much, he can't bear to be parted from him. That's quite something, considering his owner is skydiver Ron Sirull! Brutus chased Ron's plane every time he took off to make a jump, so eventually Ron took his pet with him. Brutus now jumps in a special pouch on the front of Sirull's suit, and has made over 100 sky dives since 1997.

Stitched titch

A tiny, two-week-old gosling with a broken leg was given a "bionic" limb to help it walk again. The baby goose needed teeny steel pins, bolts, and nuts to make a brace that fitted on its little leg and helped it waddle off, as good as new.

A hyena's laugh can give away its age. Hyenas don't laugh at all until they are one year old.

Best of friends

"Three little pigs" might sound like a fairytale to us, but could be a tasty snack for a tiger. However, at Sriracha Tiger Zoo in Thailand both species share a cage! The zoo has put them together to show how species can get along. The piglets sleep on the tiger's tummy, and sometimes trot around in tiger print vests, and, surprisingly, the tiger is happy to play without gobbling them up for dinner.

Gorilla gotcha

Young gorillas play games just like human children! Scientists studying these great apes have seen young gorillas sneak up on their friends and "tag" them, just like kids do in the playground. One gorilla will

THUMP!

another and then run off, waiting to be chased. And, just like humans, the adults seem too grumpy to join in, even if they are tagged.

SEW CLEVER

A nine-year-old cockatiel called Baggio can sew by holding a needle and fabric in his beak, tongue, and claws. Baggio learned his skill by watching his owner, who is a tailor, at work. He even made a TV appearance in 2004, sewing in front of the cameras. Who's a clever bird then?!

Curiosity killed the cat—and nearly finished off the horse, too! Nosy pony Gracie was found with her head stuck in a tree, and had to be cut out with a chainsaw. The poor horse pushed her head into a gap between trunk sections of a honey tree, and had to whinny for help. She was cut and bruised, and had a dislocated jaw, but recovered fine (without a trip to the "horsepital").

Ee-oogh! A starfish can pull its stomach out of its own mouth to eat with. Its tube feet move the stomach across its food to slurp it up.

Cheeky Charlie

When Charlie the chipmunk gets thirsty, he doesn't reach for a water bottle fastened to a cage. He much prefers a glass of freshly squeezed orange juice, which he sucks through a straw! When he's had enough of that, he throws out the straw and dives head-first into the glass to drink!

AMAZING ANIMALS...

Lotta lick

Everyone knows how tall giraffes are, but did you know how long their tongues are? More than a foot long—yes way! They are even long enough for a giraffe to be able to lick its own ears.

EEOOGH!

Greedy frog

The horned frog of the Amazon grows as big as a salad plate (8 inches) and eats anything that walks past it. Some dead ones have been found with half their last meal sticking out of their mouth.

Claws for thought

You would think that a cat would chase any rat brave enough to walk across its path—but not always. Two white rats and a kitten in Madras, India, became the best of friends in 2005, and played, ate, and even slept together in perfect harmony.

WOW!

Hotter otter

Sea otters live in cold waters and so have the thickest fur of all animals to keep them warm.

All dolphin teeth are the same conical shape. Some species have only four teeth, while others have up to 252.

Trashed

A pet tortoise that climbed into the trash can, looking for a warm place to hibernate, was thrown away with the rest of the household garbage—but lived to see another day. The pet survived the ride in the garbage truck, and was nearly scooped up by a bulldozer before it was found and saved from the crusher. Perhaps tortoises have nine lives, just like cats?

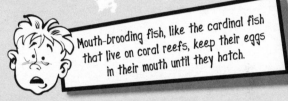

Mouth-brooding fish, like the cardinal fish that live on coral reefs, keep their eggs in their mouth until they hatch.

Big nipper

Woah! Scientists have found fossils of a giant sea scorpion that was over 8 feet long. It crawled around the ocean floor about 390 million years ago.

Super sight

A racing greyhound that never won a race has been given a new lease on life—with contact lenses! The poor dog kept coming in second as he could follow the leader, but not see the hare that guides the dogs around the track. Now the greyhound has perfect vision, and can lead the race from the front!

The big sting

More people are killed every year by jellyfish than by great white sharks.

AMAZING!

Ripley's
FEATHERLESS FASHION

1

Poor little Ralph—he's become a featherless penguin!

2

When his friends shed their feathers and grew back a new set, Ralph's fell out in a day and didn't regrow.

3

His wildlife park-keepers were so worried he would get sunburn...

4

...they made him a wetsuit from the leg of an old suit. Now he has a special suit of his own...

5

...made by a designer of dog clothes. It has his name on it and is his pride and joy.

TOILET TERROR

A four-year-old dog owner decided his muddy pup needed a wash—so he put it in the toilet bowl and flushed it! The poor pooch ended up trapped in the waste pipe for nearly four hours, and had to be rescued by plumbers. He was poked through the pipes by a Dyno-Rod® tool, so has been called Dyno by his owners. Let Dyno stay dirty next time, huh?

WHOOSH!

A death's head moth only lives for a few weeks, but while alive it can't eat or see as it has no mouth or eyes.

High and dry

You have to feel sorry for this seal. It became stranded on top of a post off the coast of Scotland, and had to wait for the tide to come back in before it could swim away to join its friends.

FARMYARD FARTS

Pher-yoo-ee! Windy animals such as cows, sheep, and goats are making the hole in the ozone layer bigger all the time. Their gas—from both ends—is methane, which is 20 times worse for the environment than the carbon dioxide produced by traffic. One cow alone can produce 88 gallon-bottles of gas every day.

Giant pandas mark their territory by performing a handstand and urinating as high as possible up the side of a tree!

Superfleas

Fleas are teeny tiny, but almost have superpowers!
They can pull

160,000 TIMES

their own bodyweight and drink 15 times their weight in blood every day. Their strength is the equivalent of a person pulling 2,670 double decker buses at the same time!

A mole 6 inches long can dig a tunnel almost 230 feet long in a single night.

SUPER PIGS

Porky performers in China took part in a special Pig Olympics in 2005! The competitors were specially trained midget pigs from Thailand, and, more recently, Pig Olympics have been staged in Russia. Thousands of human spectators watch the athletic piggies trot around a track, jump through hoops and over hurdles, play pigball, and dive into water— yes, these swine can really swim!

Since he first picked up a brush in 1998, Smithfield, a Vietnamese potbelly pig, has produced paintings so lovely that each one fetched hundreds of dollars on eBay.

The sloth sleeps upside down in a tree for three quarters of each day.

CROCCER STARS

Ever seen a crocodile in goalie gloves? Well, that's a slight exaggeration, but one man does play soccer with his pet crocs. Mexican Erroberto Piza Rios says he has tamed nearly 50 crocodiles, and takes them down to the beach for a game. Each of the crocs is named after a famous soccer player, and some of the crocs can balance the ball on their head and then roll it down their back.

A snake may be born with two heads, which will fight each other for food.

PAMPERED POOCH

Stop at a service station in Madrid, Spain, and you can get more than gas and a soda. Take your dog along for the ride and you can put it through the customized "dog wash" for as little as five dollars. Your dirty dawg will be soaped and dried before you can put your Chevy through the car wash.

Guess poo?

Want to play bingo with a difference? In some rural areas of North America they play

bingo. A field is divided into numbered squares, and the winner is the player who correctly guesses which square a cow is going to, erm, go to the toilet in.

BLESSED CREATURES

The animals went in two by two—
but not onto Noah's Ark. Instead,
once a year they head to Saint
Philip's Church in Tucson, Arizona.
There the ministers bless dogs, cats,
birds, rats, parakeets, guinea pigs,
tortoises, gerbils, snakes, lizards, and fish—
they don't actually touch the fish, just
the water! With all these animals, it's
no surprise the prayers are often
interrupted with a few barks
and squawks.

DOGGY PADDLE

Paris the sheepdog swims up to 15 miles in the Jialing River in China every day. She has been made an honorary member of the local swimming club and even has her own shower cubicle. So far she has swum over 6,500 miles.

Channel hopper

A pet rabbit in China climbs into bed with its owners every night to watch its favorite soap opera. It snuggles in between them, but is so hooked on one program, *Ms. Mermaid*, that it gets aggressive and bites the pillow if it isn't showing. The rabbit also attacks her owners if they change channels during her favorite show!

SCUBA SCHOOL

Gene Alba has not one scuba-diving pet, but two! His dog, Mutley, loves to scuba dive, but then so does his cat, Hawkeye. Unlike most cats that dislike water, Hawkeye is happy to dive straight into Gene's California pool, wearing a special suit that connects the cat's glass mask to her owner's oxygen tank. She swims around for up to an hour at a time!

LITTLE BUNDLE OF HIPPONESS

Jessica is one BIG baby—because she's a hippo! During a flood she was washed into the garden of South African game warden Tonie Joubert, and now lives with Tonie and his wife. Jessica is free to wander back to the wild, but seems to prefer home sweet home, complete with mattress and blankets for bedtime. Her best friends are the family dogs, and she loves to snack and watch TV.

SQUAWK!

Bird battle

Two parrot owners, both claiming the
right to look after the same bird, were
called to court in Florida to settle the
argument. The judge also summoned the
parrot, in case he was needed as evidence.
Tequila the parrot didn't say anything,
but did squawk when he saw the lady who
claimed to have owned him first.

Phew-y!

The spotted skunk is only half the size of the striped
skunk, but is officially the world's smelliest animal.
If it feels threatened, it will turn its back on the
threatening creature, do a handstand, and spray its
smelly liquid up to 20 feet in the air. Watch out, world!

THE LION'S SHARE

Three cats went from rats to riches when their owner died and left his money to his pets. Dr. William Grier's will gave $415,000 each to Brownie and Hellcat, and $250,000 to Charlie.

Another cat lover, Ben Rhea, left $15 million when he died, to be shared among cat charities and his own much-loved puss, Blackie. None of his human relatives got any of the loot.

Leggy-pedes

The most legs ever counted on one millipede was 750! Their name means:

"THOUSAND FEET"

but many of them have only between 100 and

300 LEGS.

A growing millipede starts with just a few legs when it is born, but every time it casts off (molts) its old skin it adds more legs!

A snow leopard can cover 50 feet of ground in a single leap.

BROWNIE

HELLCAT

HOGGING THE LIMELIGHT

Miss Piggy, a well-known competitive diving pig, shows us that pigs really can fly! The clever porker was trained how to dive and climbs the ramp to the platform herself, and then leaps off. She dived a world record 11 feet into a pool at Australia's Royal Darwin Show in 2005.

Ripley's SCARY TALE

What would you do if you heard strange noises in the street? Holden Holt, a resident of Utah, went to take a closer look and saw a pair of eyes staring at him from a storm drain.

Beavering away

Beavers have joined forces in a National Park in Alberta, Canada, to make a dam that is big enough to be seen from space! The animals themselves only grow up to 4 feet long, but several families have worked on the same dam to make it

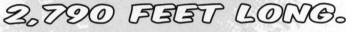

2,790 FEET LONG.

That's twice as wide as the Hoover Dam, and big enough to study on Google Earth.

A blue whale makes a noise louder than a jumbo jet. It can be heard 500 miles away underwater.

Scary stuff! Strange, too—it turns out it was a poor cow that had got stuck below street level. She was trapped there for five days while they dug her out.

BIZARRE BEASTS

Paul Springer is a farmer with a difference—he buys deformed animals and keeps them in his "stable of the strange." He first bought a six-legged calf in the 1970s, and he has since owned a cow with five legs, a pig with two snouts, and two donkeys joined at the head!

CREATURE FEATURES

Ice ice baby

Cheeky monkey Gun-mo is an ice-skating sensation! The perky primate learned to skate in just two weeks, in preparation for its performance at the 2006 Animal Academy show in Seoul, South Korea. The monkey took to the ice fully outfitted in custom-made furry skate boots and a parka with a fur-lined hood.

Sticky lick

An aardvark's favorite food is termites, and these unusual creatures have a foot-long sticky tongue to lick them up with.

INCREDIBLE!

Every gorilla's wrinkly nose is different from any other gorilla's nose, like human fingerprints.

Playing dead

Aussie is a pet fish with a difference: She swims upside down! For most fish, this is a bad sign—they're either dead or dying. Aussie, however, has been on view in a tank in a British bar for over four years, and seems perfectly happy looking at the world in her topsy-turvy way.

WOW!

A blue whale's main arteries (which carry blood around its body) are big enough for you to swim through!

Huge leap

Around 70 million years ago, the biggest frog ever known lived in Madagascar. Called the "devil frog," it grew up to 16 inches in length.

Dog on a log

Floating on a log while spinning it with your feet—or "birling," as it is called—sounds like hard work, but a Dalmatian called Peppy can stay balanced like this for an hour at a time, traveling a mile downstream! She belongs to Bill Fontana, a professional birler from Ontario, so she has learned from a master!

Easy squeezy

When a whale dives deep, it puts its skeleton under extreme pressure. Its ribs and lungs are designed to squash and collapse rather than break.

Howling chorus

A pack of 30 wolves in a Chinese zoo has been trained to sing together. Their keeper, Luo Yong, noticed that the wolves could howl in time to his guitar playing, and even pat the guitar strings with their claws.

WOOOOOOOW!

MELLOW MUTTS

Don't upset a stressed-out dog—they get moody, too. So certain yoga instructors have started classes for pets and their owners to stretch and unwind together. Yoga moves, such as the cat, the cobra, the frog, the child's pose, and the pigeon, might all appeal to Alsatians and Afghan hounds, but their favorite must be the downward-facing dog.

Groundhogs breathe only once every five minutes during periods of hibernation.

RADIO THERAPY

Two wild ponies have their own radio in their stable, to help them get used to humans. Monty and George were rescued and needed some TLC to nurse them back to health before they could be let loose again. Their keepers tuned the radio to a popular soap opera, so the ponies would become less frightened of people's voices.

friendly felines

Big-cat keeper Riana van Nieuwenhuizen is so cool with cats that she keeps several of them as pets. She lives with nine cheetahs, three leopards, a jaguar, and a lion, and has also raised tigers! They are all rescued from the wild, and share her South African home with two wolves and three dogs.

RIPLEY'S

SCAREDY BEAR

Jack, a ten-year-old tabby cat, is the best guard cat around. He's so determined to keep his yard to himself, he has even chased a bear up a tree—twice! At his New Jersey home, Jack hissed and spat at the wandering black bear as it clung to the branches. When it was brave enough to climb down, Jack followed it and forced it up a second tree for safety.

Lucky break

Lucky the duck is fortunate to be alive! She was due to be put down after breaking her leg, leaving her foot pointing in the wrong direction and making her a sitting duck for hungry foxes. Lucky for Lucky, her owner thought otherwise, and has had a special shoe made to protect Lucky's wonky webbed foot when she walks.

FIVE STAR FISH

Don't try to check into Chicago's latest hotel—it's just for fish! An area has been carefully created in the middle of the Chicago River that is shallow and rocky enough for fish to mate and mature in. It has been planted with pondweed gardens to give finned visitors somewhere to drop in and sample the luxury living conditions.

RIPLEY's
DID YOU KNOW???

The entrance to a beaver's home is underwater. When they swim, beavers have built-in "goggles," which are actually a third, see-through eyelid.

A meat-eating slug known as the ghost slug has strong, sharp teeth and eats worms like it is sucking up spaghetti.

Sharks are the only fish that can blink.

A giant anteater has no teeth, but has a tongue that can lick up ants 2 feet away, flicking in and out 160 times a minute.

Ocean plankton weighs more than all the dolphins, whales, and fish in the whole world.

The reef stonefish looks like a piece of coral but is actually deadly poisonous. It has 13 spines that inject poison into anything that touches them.